Making a Kingdom of It

Poems

Lance Larsen

University of Tampa Press

Copyright © 2024 by Lance Larsen. All rights reserved.

Manufactured in the United States of America

First Edition

On the Cover: "Under a Field of Stars," by Jacqui Larsen
Mixed media on canvas, 48" x 48"

Cover design by Ana C. Alvarado Diaz

No part of this book may be reproduced, used to train AI, stored in a retrieval system, or transmitted in any form or by any means, electronic, mechanical, photocopying, recording, or otherwise, except as may be expressly permitted by the applicable copyright statutes or in writing by the publisher.

The University of Tampa Press
401 West Kennedy Boulevard
Tampa, FL 33606

ISBN 978-1-59732-213-3 (pbk.)
ISBN 978-1-59732-214-0 (hbk.)
ISBN 978-1-59732-215-7 (ebk.)

Library of Congress Control Number:
2024940719

Browse & order online at
http://www.utampapress.org

Making a Kingdom of It

Table of Contents

One

Having My Back Erased | 1
Triage | 2
And Also I Ran | 4
Let There Be Birds | 6
Petition Ending with a Line by Rumi | 7
Blessing the Sacrament in My In-laws' Garage | 8
Why I Kissed the Dead Man | 10
Funeral Bouquet | 12
Understudy | 13
Updating My Bucket List | 14
To the Girl in Fourth Grade Who Stapled Her Arm | 15
Is Any Morning Sky Getting In? | 16
Crickets Chirring | 18

Two

I Caught an Elk Chewing | 23
Whatever Scared Hand | 24
In a Scruffy Grove | 26
Compost | 28
Singing Brokenly | 30
Pantheism for Beginners | 31
Making a Kingdom of It | 32
Once Again Morning Has Its Way with Me | 33
Upon Learning that the Last Speaker of an Amazonian Dialect has Died | 34
Widow Water | 35
Lap Swim at Rec Center Pool, 2:07 pm | 36
Self-Portrait with the State of Idaho Receding in My Rearview Mirror | 37
After a Perplexing Day, the Moon | 38
More Garter Snakes in My Theology | 39

Three

"This is Not the Hour of Poetry" | 43
Bicycles of Amsterdam | 46
Dutch Woman Riding a Tandem by Herself at Night | 48
Man Napping, Cowboy Hat over His Face, 1960 | 49
The Bread and Water of It | 50
After the Miscarriage | 52
After Reading Ecclesiastes, I Walk the Foothills in Search of Owls | 53
After Reading Song of Songs, I Take Out the Garbage | 54
Baedeker | 56
An Amateur's Guide to Holiness, Florence |57
Up to Their Dirty Wrists | 58
Happiness Memo | 60
Waiting for a Visitation | 61
Book of Salt | 62
Quail Egg | 64

Acknowledgments | 67
About the Author | 71
About the Book | 73

For Jacqui, always.

*There is always more surface to a shattered
object than a whole.*
—Djuna Barnes

My guardian angel is afraid of the dark.
—Charles Simic

*. . . pies full of secrets that even doctors don't
know, magic spell pies, smooth soothing pies
overflowing with the music of rainforests,
pies made from circles of light, pies with halos.*
—Denise Duhamel

One

Having My Back Erased

A miracle, that ride home from ER: me leaning
    forward in the passenger seat, eyes closed,
        my mother driving and drawing pictures
    on my back with her finger. Anything to distract me
from the throbbing stitches under my puffed eye.

Now a windmill, now a giraffe. I was in third grade
    and felt each gangling thing assemble, tremble
        by tremble, on the terra incognita of my skin.
    Even wrong guesses were a revelation in texture
and touch, not a comb but a rake, not a swing set

but an octopus. Then the marvelous erasing:
    just the broad warm flat of her hand. Like someone
        swabbing a deck. Or polishing it maybe. I was pure
    palimpsest, ions and vectors, a swirling energy
I hadn't yet grown into. How she turned

me into nothing. Was I floating up into sky,
    were migrating birds passing through me?
        I was ready to become whatever the sutured
    world needed me to become. Hairbrush,
T. rex, stethoscope, praying mantis, blue canoe.

Triage

My job each Friday is to decapitate the prairie
surrounding my mother-in-law's house
till it lies flat, all nap, like velvet. My other job
is to prowl the kitchen and nuzzle Jacqui
at the stove each time her mother turns her back.
Jacqui's job: push me away, keep some things
cold like yogurt and cucumbers and others hot

like yesterday's sweet and sour, and pretend
her mother's Alzheimer's will ebb away
like a pulsing migraine. I have other jobs,
like having cancer cells lasered from my face
at 3:00. Or is it 3:30? I check my phone.
Oh good, 3:30, more time to decapitate prairie,
sip juice, and swim slippery laps at the rec center.

The pool has a job: flow over me in lapping
blue waves the way Walt Whitman's beard
flows over his readers and coax me
into repeating palindromes—*Do geese see God,
rat's star, a Toyota*. Jacqui makes it official:
twenty minutes till chow and maybe I should
go mow, then nudges me out the door.

I sit my butt down on the step, and let hot
and cool battle for my body, while clouds
and a tinkling ice-cream truck scrap for my soul.
Soon the neighbor's crotch-sniffing German
shepherd sidles over. Her job is to inspect me,
ankle to chin, another private smell museum.
I take in her dagger teeth and scholarly ears.

Then she rolls to her back as if inviting me
to take her life. That's when I see the ticks
buried in her belly. Five of them, swollen
like bonus nipples in a universe painted
by Hieronymus Bosch. And she plays victim,
and I play Saint Francis of Assisi pulling
and pinching, not with tweezers but my fingers,

crushing each tick with a stray brick.
Their job is to pop, my job is to witness
and wince. And now the breeze is playing
hide-and-seek, mostly hiding, and I fire up
the mower and follow my buzzing hands
around the yard in circles, like a swimmer lost
in a wet maze, repeating *rat's star, rat's star, rat's star.*

And Also I Ran

I wheedled a ten-minute visit from the night
    nurse. This was Friday, the evening after
        my best friend hurtled through a windshield
    at 70 mph, the day before I drove
to a numbing family reunion for blue-hair aunts.
    He had a machine to track his breaths,

a tube to collect pee, and a pair of legs
    that would never again shuffle or glide or dance.
        I was fifteen plus four months, and my friend
    was fifteen plus blood all over the Ford
Bronco, even on the road, even on trees.
    Promise me, he said, that you'll definitely check

out the crash site. And I said no, not
    one part of me wants to see blood on trees.
        Every six hours his Stryker bed flipped him
    like a flapjack, stomach down for now,
with a cutout for his face, so I sprawled
    on the floor. Days before, we had lain on grass,

close as sleeping bags, counting stars
    and girlfriends we didn't have. Tonight, more
        of the same bull, and less. His chin and my dirty
    shoes trading gossip, the eighty-seven stitches
on his back giving me the silent treatment,
    the moon outside skinny dipping in the fountain.

Before leaving, I touched my friend's good shoulder,
    warmish like when you put your arm around a girl
        at a matinee. And the hum of machines was a prayer
    to healing, and dirty tiles were a prayer to grit,
and my friend saying *Hey, man, later*, was amen.
    Outside, sprinklers did a silvery dance with the grass.

I broke into a run then, sliding through chain
    link to an endless empty parking lot. With so many
        overhead lights I had three shadows at once,
    like three wavery souls. When I ran they moved,
one pinning me to pavement, one sliding
    off like oily water, one being born up ahead.

What did I care? When I closed my eyes
    they went away. Just a buzzing breeze
        and these slabs called legs doing their work.
    They didn't want to run. My lungs pushed
them, my slippery beating heart, and my friend's
    catheter leaking amber bubbles in room 514.

Who needed a soul, or the disappearing shadow
    of a soul? Breath was enough, and hurrying
        blood, provided it stayed inside me. Nine-thirty
    at night, the day after and the day before.
A clean, brisk, heavy, terrifying, innocent
    Friday in June. I ran and ran and also I ran.

Let There Be Birds

Me and the pond, me and a trail and the pond,
me and a sky tattered with clouds and the pond—
and over two hundred geese ringing the water.
I've come here to disappear into November air,
geese the catalyst, geese on loan from Alberta
and migrating to Chihuahua, very modern looking,

black and white and winterbourne gray, a honking
art installation with wings. On weekdays,
I'm a teacher, taxpayer, vacuumer of dusty rugs,
REM junkie wearing yesterday's socks, but here,
each Sunday, I'm a murderer. So think the geese.
With each step I take, two or three plump

into the shallows and schooner away atop
this bright and scummy mirror. All because
I've transformed this path into a stomping
ground, my legs devotion, my breath a broken
psalm. Look at me, guardian of feather
and beak, coaxing wild birds into dark water.

Look at me, an amiable ox. Hundreds of miles
till these birds cross the Rio Grande
and honk in Spanish. If there's a god blessing
this mess, picture a five-year-old holding
a crayon who says let there be birds, let there be
bliss, then adds curlicues of sun to a puffing lake.

Petition Ending with a Line by Rumi

Angels of this world, I grow tired of my sloshing
blood, my tomahawk nose that splits the day
in half. I want to dip my face in a river and feel
underwater grass flowing like a mermaid combing
out her hair. I caught a trout and ate it, caught

a trout and said thank you river, thank you
caddisflies, but I wasn't transformed into a fish.
When will I grow a dorsal fin and dark gills?
I began in a far galaxy. Why was I pulled
into this world of forceps and a woman's cries?

I want to sip mist and taste eternity, open
my mouth and polish off a floating cloud or two.
Give me squirming eels instead of a shirt,
owls instead of a diploma, crickets instead of
a cell phone. Let a street magician juggle moons

where my heart used to be. And now some dark
colloquium of the blood starts up. Has the next
world already arrived? I'll count in fireflies, let stars
be my abacus. Where, where will it take me,
this bender that began in some other tavern?

Blessing the Sacrament in My In-laws' Garage

I wear a paper mask, Jacqui a festive Aloha number,
and ten feet away, card table between us,
sit her parents, both in their nineties, maskless,
too hard to explain to them pandemic risks,
and we're listening to "All Creatures
of Our God and King" on Jacqui's phone.
To keep Covid at bay we use the garage
to bow our heads and lift Jesus to our mouths.
I close the garage door for privacy and open
the back door to coax a breeze playing hard to get.
This is the eucharist, Utah style, with me
preparing bread and water, me kneeling
on concrete, and me passing to a congregation
of three, then taking a scrap myself.
The garbage can, big as a witch's cauldron, squats
behind my left shoulder, shovels and rakes
line the wall like saints, and three boxes
of slug bait on the shelf haven't killed anything,
with or without bones, since before 9-11.
We curse dementia and downplay pandemic.
Never mind that whole countries have evaporated
from my in-laws' memory banks, goodbye
Thailand, so long Peru, also farewell to continental
drift and Bay of Pigs and the faces of three
adult grandchildren who visited at New Year's.
No more Harriet Tubman or Ruth Bader
Ginsberg, though Fred Astaire still kindles
something—wait, wasn't he a general?
Jesus, though, is still here, not homemade
or Wonder but a torn English muffin, and soon
he'll be four trickles of water in Dixie cups.
He's summer solstice, our longest day
and shortest night. He's robin and finch
and sometimes an elegant Steller's jay ricocheting
tree to tree. He's the hoe that can chop

weeds till sunset and the broom that sweeps
away mouse droppings and crumbs,
and He's this sweet tangle of silver white
lights we'll drape over the flocked tree
come Christmas. Monkey wrench and vice
grips, Selah, tape measure and twine, Selah.
And He's the dusty blue cruiser bike, tires
still good, hanging from rafters, ready
at any instant to ferry us to what comes next.
Till then, we bow our heads to this glorious
broken now and we ask and we ask and we ask.

Why I Kissed the Dead Man

Because he took a final breath but the sky
    went on and on, because the nurse turned
        off the machines, because he was my
father-in-law, because I loved his daughter
    Jacqui and she kissed him first and I wanted
        to kiss whatever she kissed, because the skin

on his neck and face were still warm,
    because I loved him from afar the way
        one loves oily reliable tools and stories
about designing Cold War sonar smarter
    than God, because love has sink holes
        in it lost rivers disappearing into the Delphic

earth then returning freshened 10,000 years
    later, because he spent his last weeks
        shredding things junk mail canceled checks
yellowed engineering books page by page
    little metallic teeth digesting his life,
        because he had seven full trash bags

squirreled away in his bedroom and hoped
    to walk them to the curb himself,
        because wouldn't it be lovely to toss
that confetti off the hospital roof and let
    a ferocious wind dust the city with pieces
        of him, because I hoped to save Jacqui

from everything dark and intractable
    and human and sour but couldn't,
        because there were unmapped continents
in her kiss and a hidden waterfall,
    because there was only electrician's tape
        in mine and wire snips and once

an impromptu trip to buy a smoke detector,
    because fathers are so damned hard to love
        and fathers-in-law harder,
because I wanted and still want someone
    to kiss me after I die, someone with three
        days' growth of beard who doesn't have to.

Funeral Bouquet

Tomorrow these lilies and mums will dress
cemetery dirt and brace up the sky—

and bid passing angels to roost like crows
on the sagging shoulders of mourners.

But tonight they sit on a kitchen slab
witnessing the sacraments of how we go on.

Here twilight and a pot of soup
boiling over, here broccoli and charred

leeks in the pan, here wilting greens
glistening with vinegar and oil,

here thyme, here tap water in chipped cups,
here a derelict cook checking on rolls

that won't rise, here a cat jumping
from floor to counter to lick a buttery fork.

Understudy

I'm pointing to faded snapshots of her grandchildren
and sounding out their names, syllable by syllable.
All these children came out of me? my mother-in-law
asks. Each day dementia maroons her
on a new island. No, I say, out of your daughter.

And now I'm pointing to destinations that have
evaporated overnight: mother-in-law riding
an elephant in Thailand, mother-in-law crossing
a footbridge in the Andes made of grass
and llama spit. *I had houses in all these places?*

No, I say, but you visited once. Her mind
is a tumbleweed tumbling but she can still belt
out *Jolly Old St. Nick*. This is how she copes,
never mind she's months and several holidays
out of whack. She nods off, and I let her.

I'm no medic or deep-trauma therapist,
just a washer of milky cups and keeper
of the thermostat. He who retrieves junk mail
from the freezer, frozen peas from the dryer,
he who hides pills in cherry yogurt and spoons

them into her mouth. Also a workaday sage
who remembers the old cures, like throwing open
a window. Let raw sunlight cleanse a dying
room, remind the world and me that the cool
mercy washing over us is called a breeze.

Updating My Bucket List

A few successes. Climb Huayna Picchu, check.
    Howl at howler monkeys in the Amazon, check.
        Play "Corcovado" on my own second-hand grand,
    check, though it sounds more like Chopsticks
than bossa nova. Still haven't played blackjack
    naked or jumped from a Cessna. Just scratch
        those two? Also I've failed to judge between
    button mushrooms and destroying angels
on a drowsy morning in Colorado, cook up
    the former with garlic and lemon and a dash
        of paprika and nibble them on a veranda in Telluride.
    Nor have I made it through *Anna Karenina*
just yet, not even a bad translation,
    though I feel I grasp her infidelity, that is if
        a coastal breeze can comprehend a cyclone.
    We're all just smelly squatters stuck here
for seven decades give or take. Haven't tasted
    Ouzo or rented a limo for a Stones concert,
        never ran with the bulls at Pamplona.
    Scratch those too, more macho bluster?
Isn't the point of bucket lists to prove we're still
    alive, curious and fallible and filled with dumb
        longing, like a puppy trying to make friends
    with a Roomba? No cool tattoos yet, and I've never
been jailed, though I once fell asleep in a park
    beside the Thames and woke when a bobby
        kicked my foot. What an honor to be
    mistaken for a vagrant not a tourist!
I stretched and said, Thank you dark sky.
    And to pigeons, which are derelict angels grubbing
        for crumbs, Hell, we've had a good run,
haven't we?—even you motley ones missing toes.

To the Girl in Fourth Grade Who Stapled Her Arm

I don't remember her name only that she stapled
her arm five times then rolled down her sleeve
to hide the evidence. The day before,
I killed a bird. All morning I watched the hand
of that stapled arm spell *gristle* and *patriot* and do
times tables. Something about nerve damage

when she was little, something about no pain,
so why not staple between elbow and wrist?
The bird was a robin, bb gun not even mine.
At the pencil sharpener, Staple Girl
showed us the punctures, which didn't bleed,
only oozed a little, like oil, under her sleeve.

At lunch, we followed her to the monkey bars.
Thank you blue pen cap, which she wriggled
back and forth till each staple popped free.
Thank you toilet paper, which she used for
dabbing. Thank you sky for going along with it,
and pennies in my pocket, which I could jingle.

I only wanted to scare that robin. It flipped
from the tree and twitched in tall grass.
Thank you Staple Girl for showing us
how to hurt the body before lunch then sing
to your wounds by playing Foursquare.
How could I sing to wings that didn't move?

Was the world stapled together by secrets?
Seven times seven and recess and dirty clouds
and regret. Wounded arm and spelling quiz
hand. Finger on the trigger, stilled bird on the grass.
Hopscotch in this life, dark psalms in the next?
Flag doing nothing patriotic with its rippling stripes.

Is Any Morning Sky Getting In?

Beginner's kiss, windstorm kiss, kiss my nose kiss,
crash kiss, pesto and blue corn chips kiss,
that was the summer you tracked them all,
the summer we flunked driver's ed
so we walked everywhere, like vagabonds
we walked, like barefoot children we walked,
I was Aries and you were second trombone,
you were Gemini, the birthday girl,
and I was mow the widow's lawn every Thursday,
lemonade kiss, lip gloss kiss, good news
barbecue kiss, that was the summer
of shortcuts, through backyards and over
fences, the summer your cousin took
his life but you didn't tell me for weeks,
the kisses growing softer and sadder,
penguin kiss, balcony kiss, hurry hide
from the cops kiss, and we crossed the river
by stones and jumped on the trampoline
you called Blue Spaceship, then finally
your cousin's story fell from your mouth,
his failed meds, the rowboat across the pond,
the terrible waterskiing rope, then rain fell
on us, and kisses followed, crying kiss,
hello I'm the lost girl kiss, just be with me kiss,
I touched you but you didn't touch back,
I was tennis shoes and sunburn,
you were sandals and grass in your hair,
then a black dog circled the trampoline,
was this a sign, you asked, my cousin adored
big sloppy pooches, so we climbed down,
you tousled his ears then gave me
a falling star kiss, and I shook the dog's paws
and gave you a welcome back to the world
kiss, that was the summer you moved
to Michigan, the summer before I got

my license and gave up on walking,
the summer you said I'm trying to believe
in everything, reincarnation, henna, stuffing
letters to the departed in a bottle and throwing
them off Buffalo Cliff, and I asked
is it working, is any morning sky getting in,
and you said, there are kisses we've never
dreamed of, and later we invented
them, the peach kiss, the Ouija board kiss,
the wade under the bridge barefoot kiss,
the kiss until the dead say to stop kissing kiss.

Crickets Chirring

In fifth grade I was sure I had a soul,
but Gracie Millsap, whom I clocked
with a snowball on St. Patrick's
Day, said I didn't. I've been wondering
for fifty years, looking for my broken
face in rain puddles, brooding
on piers and stalled elevators,
grilling from afar indifferent stars.
Everyone resorts to something.
The widow wanders the city,
pushing two foofy dogs in a stroller
and we let her. The marathoner
carries his mother's ashes in a baggie
against his thigh and we let him.
A wasp lays her eggs inside a swaying
caterpillar on my porch, so her children
will wake to a little snack, and I let her.
And angels let her, and wings
and instinct and a short summer
conspire to let her. Each of us carries
a lit fuse or a swallowed compass
pointing north. Everyone driven
to arrive, hoping to kiss God
on his radiant mouth or be swept up
into tantalizing mist. Some read
Ecclesiastes to make the journey
darker, some watch cigarette smoke
worm its way toward the sublime.
Meanwhile, another homeless
man jerry-rigs a lean-to under
the bridge out of extension cords
and stolen pallets and listens
to country songs deep into the night.
If solstice begins with a coyote's howl,
sometimes it ends with a ballad

by Dolly Parton. Tonight, teens
will park above the city, as they always
do, and the mayor will let them,
and the night cop texting the waitress
will let them, and Ursa Major
and Ursa Minor will sign release forms
letting them. That craggy moon:
real estate these teens hope to own
one day, their first kiss a down payment.
Soon enough their souls will grow
bored. Maybe his will frog
its way to the pulsing swamp.
Maybe hers will swoop, bat-like,
reading the dark like a book
about buggy heaven. Meanwhile
their stranded beautiful bodies
will be left to learn by braille and grief
and crickets chirring that none
of us was meant to live here for long.

Two

I Caught an Elk Chewing

And she caught me chuffing up the trail
and we locked eyes—hello mystery,
hello hallelujah and kingdom come.
All day I've carried her like a prayer, down
the mountain and into my kitchen, up
the stairs and into my den, with me
while shaving, with me running the day's
humdrum errands. The trail was steep,
night had rolled up its tattered bedroll
with all its stars, and she was eating
arrow leaf balsamroot like candy.
I will speak nothing but elk all day
and chew greens with abandon,
elk on the brain, elk in my devotions.
Tonight I will dream her anew, not
as hunters do, my finger on a trigger,
a buck knife on my belt. I'll dream her
in a clearing, her on one side, me
on the other, moonlight falling between
us like silver rain. How many miles
will she cover by nightfall? Where
will she sleep? Others, no doubt,
have glimpsed her but not locked eyes
as I did or picked up elk scat three months
ripe and watched it fleck away like spores,
then walked home, a widower. Watch
her jaws working, her fierce high plains
face tilted in first light, eyes wet,
her big elk mouth powdered with pollen.

Whatever Scared Hand

    The deer was dead and now Bus Driver Lady
was standing in the aisle, saying she had never hit
    a creature before and was godawful sorry
        and felt it all over, indicating not just
    her heart but her black lace boots and trembling
shoulders, even her hair. Yes, the deer was dead
    but that didn't change her *numero uno*

    priority: get us from Sad Point A
to Less Sad Point B, on schedule, more or less,
    that is if the damned traffic cooperated for once.
        The deer was dead but morning
    was still gorgeously September. Did the maples
on the hill seem more like rust or cleansing
    fire? I tried to keep score by staring at the leaves

    but fire would win then rust then fire again.
The deer was dead. Still, geese angled
    across the sky like an adoring caress,
        and a hot air balloon hung above a cornfield
    advertising that now you, yes you, have
a friend in the diamond business.
    The deer was dead and the blind woman

    two rows up dropped her hand from her lap
to the aisle, and her black lab licked her fingers.
    She brought her hand close to her face
        and sniffed. Who knew that the smell
    of dog saliva could bring comfort?
The deer was dead and now Bus Driver
    Lady glided up the aisle to her driver's chair.

Then turned back towards us. *One more thing,
whose bike is strapped to the nose of the bus?* My hand
    shot up like a third grader with the wrong answer.
        I had forgotten all about my bike.
    She looked at me. *The good news is your bike
will be fine*, she said, *just splashes of you know
    what from the deer on the tires, maybe on the seat.*

I have some Windex, she said, *I'll give it
to you later at your stop.* Was it supposed to console
    me that the bus was the murder weapon, my bike
        only a passive witness? Either way the deer
    was already roadkill. The heroic black lab
two rows up turned around against its better
    training, and looked us over, me over, waiting

    to lick whatever scared hand the world offered up.

In a Scruffy Grove

My friend hid the jug of Mogen David
in a scruffy grove of sagebrush
behind his house his mom was Greek
Orthodox his dad all muscles
and moustache also a shoulder surgeon

my friend hid the bottle under
two tumbleweeds three burlap sacks
he pulled it out like a priest unwrapping
a statue shake it he said so I did
now unscrew the lid and sniff so I did

his mom was bipolar his dad worked
Sunday ski patrol not wine inside
but piss the kid kind collected
from a fifth grader in a hurry between
episodes of *Gilligan's Island* and *I Dream*

of Jeannie his mom kept falling asleep
by day his dad had a girlfriend
in Sun Valley why hoard your own pee
my friend didn't know maybe drown
spiders or spike punch maybe trick kids

dumber than us into taking a swig
were there kids dumber than us
Hell why couldn't my dad drive
a Porsche or golf at the country club
let me pee into your bottle I said

nope my friend said it has to be me
go twenty feet away and play lookout
he said if I dribble this nasty brew
on pictures of my enemies and pray
maybe I can make terrible things happen

his mom played "Claire de lune"
eyes closed and looked beautiful
and half dead his dad tall as a tower
my friend was eleven and turning
into a kid who hurts cats for fun

I was ten and would soon master
floating above the city I could
already feel my invisible wings
budding forth it was a good year April
or maybe May tincture of fifth grade

my friend's mom baked spare change
into birthday cupcakes if you bit a quarter
you were chosen his dad swore a lot
f bombs going off inside my head
everything flowed into everything else

me watching my friend my friend learning
by the burning at the tip of all he was
how to conquer sagebrush how to play
at being a man how to leak and leak
into the world till the green bottle is full

Compost

I sing the dreck we make a feculent muck
of saving the kingdom come of clipped

grass whirligig leaves and deadheaded
daylilies Parrot Moon kissing Primal Scream

all mixed with the god forbid of kitchen scraps
corn cobs like the chewed legs of pigs

tomatoes sluicy with vegetal roe the mosh-pit
hair of pineapples topped and here a scatter

of artichoke leaves like a dismembered
armadillo fortune cookies minus the fortune

enough cat kibble to punctuate Ezekiel
sumpy cantaloupes ripe as betrayal

not to mention spent tissues sopped
in sneezes and nosebleeds Sunday papers fat

with want ads and exposés here an au pair
who tutors trig and scrubs bidets here a hung

jury jiggered by bribes all of it layered
with bales of peat trucked from Alberta bogs

each week I turn it each week I lift my pitchfork
to decay the ripeness almost intestinal

I'm making a bed for Osiris all things reeky
folded together stars falling nightly

from myth into loam in the shaded heat
of this plot a pair of salamanders twining

striped with fire moist as adultery
steam rising with what is buried like plumes

of heat escaping the dead how do I channel
such desire now I kneel and now

I warm my hands in this funk solstice
and dross offal and equinox if only

this sweet god of rot would hold her breath
if only she'd stop panting my name

Singing Brokenly

at least once a week drink straight
from the tap a reminder of your
animal DNA and how one day
we'll all be married to air
a slinking cat can help measure
a room's fault lines and teach you
how to hide wounds in plain sight
to taste betrayal cut your finger
and let it bleed into your curious
mouth some call this atavistic
some call this good therapy
count on one rainstorm per picnic
one moon rising behind a helter-
skelter skyline of shedding trees
one magpie singing brokenly
who needs more than this
one assassin spider in your shower
cleaning its legs like a violinist
rosining up for a sonata
how many times have you died
since waking every garden is a grave
every hand beholden to five
fingerling gods don't count days
sing minutes how would you dance
if a cloud were your partner
how would you kiss this tulip
if your lips were a teasing breeze

Pantheism for Beginners

The sky is blue enough to drown in,
this cloud floating over the cul-de-sac
the best grief counselor in weeks,
its shade more layered than rehab:
a place to loaf and sift. I toss
pinecones at the fence to scare away
the yawning abyss in the middle
of the day. I stand up three times
and three times my shadow follows
suit! How I love obedience—
also gravity. One shoe on in case
I need to save another garter snake
from my patrolling cat, one shoe
off so I blend in, *au naturel*,
with fallen leaves and this errant
pair of ants dragging a dead cricket
back to the club house. This aspen
grove is a library, each book open
to the same fluttery page. Soon
I'll turn over a stone and trade
summer for fall, save the howl
of a dog in a bottle, touch
toadstools sprouting from what's
left of a dove. A windfall peach
teaches me what to do next: kneel,
blow off pollen and gnats and grit,
take a bite without using my hands.

Making a Kingdom of It

nights so cold we wore hunting shirts
to bed and rogue porcupines

snuffled in from the foothills
to munch fallen pears moonlight sliding

around the cabin like a pickpocket
I've been away months Lord

if not years and she's been gone longer
warm me with this sputtery fire

Lord or with your oh so fulsome
breath like that Lord yes and like this

Once Again Morning Has Its Way with Me

as in this quartet of ants ferrying a torn
moth across snail slime and slate

as in my wife's shirt belling and blooming
on the breezy line teal against teal

as in this stray cat after my run licking
five miles of salty questions from my leg

Upon Learning that the Last Speaker of an Amazonian Dialect Has Died

I junked the junk mail deadheaded a gallica rose
blew crushed leaves into the wind
in protest then picked up a windfall pear
and ate around the wormhole
still the sky did not make a place
in its blue bosom for that lonely speaker
his first syllables did not climb above the canopy
like hallowed smoke and circle the world
seven times in a gaggle of endangered toucans
no one translated his final sentence
into Indo-European or Latin or old French
or even mongrel American
it was a Tuesday or a Friday shadows crept
out of the anthill an earthworm with more hearts
than a tentful of grieving girls tendrilled
forth then retreated I listened to the nothing
that was outside and declared it good
and the nothing that was inside
and it was better we are always naming things
with or without words then everyday noises
came back a lawnmower a school bus
disgorging feral children a lone dog barking

Widow Water

All summer, garden snakes slithered in and out
of her grief. Now she has Canada geese to count,

as they angle south for the season. The lake
is empty of wings, reminding her how ice first

honors edges, how inky skies honor where
he drowned. At night, she makes and unmakes

the bed but never sleeps in it. By day, the leaves
don't fall fast enough so she walks under

the maple, banging branches with a rake. Gloves?
She lost them weeks ago during a midnight

ramble, so now she wears his hunting socks
on her hands, wool with red stripes. She saves

his whiskers in a shaving mug, clipped fingernails
rolled up in an old bra, little fixes that fix

nothing. She used to scatter mums on waves
but grew tired of watching them serenely float.

Now she lobs one of his hammers or a handful
of screws, each splash a little gulp, a thank you.

On the couch tonight she'll light his last cigarette
and let it smolder down to ash while she eats

a pomegranate, jewel by bleeding jewel, smoke
tonguing the wall like a spirit seeking release.

Lap Swim at Rec Center Pool, 2:07 pm

Bless all eight lanes, the five taken and the three calling my name.
Bless today's brave consortium of thrashing limbs.
Bless steamed-up windows and echoey tiles, and this recipe of stinks:
    sweat, wet towels, deodorant, musky gym bags . . .
Bless how I throw myself in, not like a seal but a rusty boat anchor.
Bless bodies in bad swimsuits, how water strives to eroticize
    everything but fails.
Bless my klutzy sidestroke, which is how I warm up.
Bless pool light: greenish and smeared and small-town transcendental.
Bless my breath and keep blessing it so I don't drown.
Bless city taxes I pay to share this water with strangers.
Bless leaky bladders during kiddie lessons, and the chlorine
    the punk lifeguard dumps in afterwards to even things out.
Bless these buoys making me mayor of my own shimmery country.
Bless Old Man Leiberman kvetching again in lane 7, Yiddish words
    I didn't know I knew piling up in my head.
Bless schlemiel, klutz, schlep, putz around, do *all* personify me?
Bless the greats, like Gertrude Ederle, all sheep grease and fire,
    who swam the English Channel in 1926, shattering every record.
Bless the watery words that recite me: "There's a certain slant
    of light / on winter afternoons / that oppresses like . . . "
Bless all things that float: bugs, bubbles, Band-aids, my bunkum
    thoughts about the next life.
Bless the Dow inching up, the Tao (in me at least) spiraling down.
Bless how slow I swim: uno dos tres, Able Baker Charlie Dog,
    the story of Sartre hiding in his sister's closet after winning the Nobel.
Bless gills, which I wish I had.
Bless my ex-neighbor, Cynthia Truett in her tenty orange suit grousing
    that it's too cold to jump in, Cynthia who once rescued
    a baby fox from a window well using her own crutch.
Bless the three mosquito bites above her left ankle.
Bless how she bends to scratch them like one of Degas's blue dancers.

Self-Portrait with the State of Idaho Receding in My Rearview Mirror

Few of my faults will shake the world.
I too am landlocked and wish
I had a navy. My caves drip with dark
knowing. My arches have fallen,
my swamps gather the strangest of birds.
Estuaries? Got 'em. Hot spots
and sinkholes? Too many to count.
My Lost River lips the sky then slips
underground and simmers in secret
give or take an ice age. If only
all my boundaries were straight,
if only they didn't squiggle like snakes.
Ain't no one nohow gonna lift me
by my panhandle. At night I fill with tales
of Bigfoot sightings and old gold.
At first light animal sadness seeps in,
like mist, and sometimes stays.
My craters resemble the moon.
Beyond this point, no motorized vehicles.
Beyond this point, take off your shoes.
My horizons? Keep squinting.
One day Sacagawea will return
from the north and lead me home.
My badlands were once bedrock.
I have wild places not even God
has visited. People I love keep passing
through on their way to somewhere else.

After a Perplexing Day, the Moon

More slippery than Sappho, more earthy
than Eve. Trout jump to kiss her,
then fall back like spent rockets.
Tonight she's brie, tomorrow an aged
gorgonzola. Her workers work graveyard.
She naps in dirty puddles then flits
across town to brighten midnight
martinis at the pier. Women carry her
gossip in their wombs. She's a flashlight
to the fearful, a chalice to believers,
an accomplice to murderers digging
impromptu graves. The more we drink,
the more she dances like Mick Jagger,
all swagger and sway. The lost tribes
nestle in her craters, sleeping off
diaspora. When she combs her blue hair,
dogs howl for the next life. She floats
above our sadness, bright as a jellyfish.

More Garter Snakes in My Theology

What a lousy citizen of the republic I am.
I pay my garbage fees on time
but never throw away half enough stuff.
No taxidermied creatures festoon
my wall, only clean sheds hanging
from my flimsy pear tree—ghosts of elk
and deer auditioning for reincarnation.
My idea of politics equals reading
Blake while sipping a mango smoothie.
On licentious days, I read him
in my underwear. I need more voodoo
in my mortgage payments, more garter
snakes in my theology—time to nap
naked on a hot apocalyptic rock.
When I next cross a snail trail I'll compose
a haiku to the small house movement,
how to slide your life along on a sled
of lubricious spit. If a destroying
angel swoops in, I'll shrug my shoulders:
Fine, take me, but can I choose the play list?
I'm sitting on my floor in my pajamas.
It's All Hallow's Eve, a misty morning:
three avocadoes ripen on the sill,
my cat sacked out, as if re-charging
for a night of haunting. My granddaughter,
dressed as a witch, is dragging a pair
of rattly plastic skeletons up the stairs.
Bones walking, she yells, *bones walking!*

Three

"This is Not the Hour of Poetry"

    For Adam Zagajewski (1945-2021)

These the words you shared on a Friday
           at noon with an audience of two hundred,
      then read your poems anyway. Your voice
a brash witness to the mutilated world.
           Late October, safe in the Rocky Mountains.

Not the hour of poetry, not the hour to be seduced
           by the smells of Poland, its strong coffee
      and weak tea, its alleys and chickens beheaded
in backyards. And we were not seduced.
           We could have been doing Pilates instead,

napping in carrels, or stapling small thing A
           to large thing B. We should have taken you
      at your word like good seminarians and bumbled
our way to the exit. After all, who can suss out
           meaning from a cowering poem at noon?

"This is not the hour of poetry." I repeated
           your words to myself, in half agreement.
      But, if not now, Adam, then when—
must we wait till midnight? Or is twilight better, day dissolving
           into mist, and does good verse necessarily follow?

Must we wear a raffish scarf and channel
           continental thought? We sank deeper into our chairs
      and tried to amp up our animal hungers,
listening now with our skin and hair, taking
           in your images: pigeons fouling windowsills,

strangers waiting for trains, the sky scribbled
                with smoke, untuned pianos drinking our grief.
           Also cut flowers in some plaza, a drifty sweetness
almost primeval. Had we left, we might have
                sipped a Coke, crammed for a quiz, ghosted an ex.

Instead something caught. We took off
                our vagabond shoes and wriggled our toes
           in hopes of pilgrimage. Some fuse burning
inside us. True, we had no business practicing
                mysticism for beginners or trading bodies

with a hungry owl coursing a field. We had searched
                our hearts and parsed the difference
           between loneliness and solitude: were we ready now
to close our eyes and entertain the mysteries?
                Maybe noon was the hour of poetry after all.

All the spunky verbs crawled out from under
                rocks, nouns pulsed and multiplied
           like manna, and adjectives, once forbidden,
were everywhere again, quickfire fireworks!
                Metaphors lit up history and bid us stare

at the gulag, and pogrom, into the burning
                church of our own bodies. Late Beethoven
           was there to help. And Osip Mandelstam.
Wasn't the search the thing? That was poetry.
                And you at the podium, and us shouldering

the sadness of East Europe. That was poetry too.
                Your mouth moving, our mouths savoring
           and gulping, savoring and gulping.
Your caesuras tugged at us. We could almost,
                I swear, taste your tantalizing enjambments

and white space. Pauses everywhere.
                Was Jerusalem tucked away at the end
        of a line? Were our hearts broken yet?
Was that God sitting in a dingy café in Warsaw
                dreaming of us, steam rising from a blue cup?

Bicycles of Amsterdam

New bikes, rusty bikes, all of them slick
    with rain, one rider in a burka and high heels,
        one in yoga pants, one wearing a green poncho.
I like how the Dutch think: who needs putt-putt
    golf or capital punishment, we have bikes, who needs
        nuclear missiles, we have bikes. And me without a bike.

In seventh grade I had a crush on Anne
    Frank and now that doomed hopeful rainy
        feeling is back, it rains up, it rains sideways,
but maybe this time she'll escape, it rains
    as if God himself were going door to door.
        My parents are long dead so I shouldn't feel

like an orphan, especially with rivers
    of bikes sliding by, one bike made of wood,
        another flamingo pink with crochet, but I do.
No one is calling to ask if I arrived safely,
    no one tracking me on GPS, do I even exist?
        Bikes dark and muddy as stallions, call that one

Medieval Sadness, call this one Apocalypse,
    dark in an honest postmodern way,
        riders always carrying two kinds of cargo,
inner and outer, yogurt and *Does my beloved truly*
    love me?, grabber screws and *I hope I don't miscarry again.*
        Me, I'm still a rotten little pedestrian, inner

and outer folded into one because I'm carrying
    only myself: *Anne Frank, where are you? Let us be*
        orphans together. If I were a bike, I'd live
in Holland, if I were a slobbery mutt I'd ride
    in the bright basket of a Dutch widow and drink
        air like a pirate, everything tidy and brisk,

bikes there, walkers here, and cars like dinosaurs stuck
    in traffic. Miraculous isn't it, a city where a bike
        is faster than a taxi? Just aim your toes and heartache
across town. Dutch bikes are like love affairs,
    if you slow down, you'll tip over so keep pedaling,
        holding your face to the rain like a tulip opening.

Dutch Woman Riding a Tandem by Herself at Night

is darkness her escort is she ferrying God
no one seated behind her but a scrape of wind
ghost pedals pedaling under a brimming sky
tomorrow my mother will be dead one year

no one seated behind her but a scrape of wind
I'm an orphan on vacation a son heavy with home
tomorrow my mother will be dead one year
this empty seat a reminder this frieze of rain

I'm an orphan on vacation a son heavy with home
I carry stories disguised as Gouda and bread
this empty seat a reminder this frieze of rain
I forgot the bananas should I buy more tea

I carry stories disguised as Gouda and bread
she has turned the corner vanishing into mist
I forgot the bananas should I buy more tea
the canal burbles on all purl and slosh

she has turned the corner vanishing into mist
is a lover waiting or a child with a broken arm
the canal burbles on all purl and slosh
a glistening hymn I'll hum all the way home

is a lover waiting or a child with a broken arm
ghost pedals pedaling under a brimming sky
a glistening hymn I'll hum all the way home
is darkness her escort is she ferrying God

Man Napping, Cowboy Hat over His Face, 1960

sun streaming in like some Old West visitation
my dad poses as a cowboy in a ghost town
make it June or July I have not yet been born
leaning back feet propped on a pot-bellied stove

my dad poses as a cowboy in a ghost town
hundreds of dead calendars hold up the wall
leaning back feet propped on a pot-bellied stove
his boots the color of mud hands like leather

hundreds of dead calendars hold up the wall
is he cowhand or outlaw? JFK assassination not yet
his boots the color of mud hands like leather
will men walk on the moon? will I have a mom?

is he cowhand or outlaw? JFK assassination not yet
they have spent all spring trying to make me
will men walk on the moon? will I have a mom?
Kent State not yet Aquarius not yet I'm waiting

they have spent all spring trying to make me
is my dad asleep? Only me dreaming him alive
Kent State not yet Aquarius not yet I'm waiting
God could be sneaking a smoke under a tree

is my dad asleep? Only me dreaming him alive
make it June or July I have not yet been born
God could be sneaking a smoke under a tree
sun streaming in like some Old West visitation

The Bread and Water of It

After the torn scraps of sacrament bread
came paper thimbles of water,
warmish and straight from the tap,
which turned into whatever light
or blood filled your head. The tray
moved hand over hand, pew by pew,
slow as faith. Outside, the snow piled

high then higher, all snarl and swarm.
I was a smart-ass thirteen, and my frayed
taciturn father was fifty-two,
and we had growled at each other
that morning and the night before,
and both of us, stewing in our stormy
huffs, needed to be chastised and dressed

down, washed and welcomed home,
in the calm and creep of it, the savvy sip
and savor of it. I drank first,
then he tipped his wet cup to his lip,
eyed me, then poured the rest
on my wrist, a gesture that dripped
somehow of both tantrum and truce.

This was not the upper room and inn
of it, but some backward Idaho
I'm sorry thirst of it, a thirst for what
we couldn't name, and we watched
that splotch on the cushion bloom red,
then redder, and my father was trickster
pleased, and I was lost-son relieved.

And we never spoke of it, the pith
and path, the gallery and gulf and game
of it, Jesus soaking into the wet
nap. My father cleared his throat,
and I rearranged my Sunday bones,
scooting close enough to him to hide
that lovely stain between us with my thigh.

After the Miscarriage

We grew more baby hungry than ever—
and more deliberate. More like junior

scientists converting their ratty bed
into a lab than like lovers trying to chase

stars across the sky. Call it coupling
by calendar and clock. We still had room

for musk and mist and licking breezes
lit by jazz, but we were makers now, gene

splicers, driven by the braille and breath
of what if, the slippery abracadabra of we.

After Reading Ecclesiastes, I Walk the Foothills in Search of Owls

I stumble through a mess of gnats holding
mass and swallow two or three, then settle

on a rotting stump and make dusk my desk.
Nothing new under the sun, says the Preacher.

How about this moon? If it didn't shine
like a searchlight it might scowl like a skull.

No owls tonight, no shadows of owls.
Just a magpie winging away like a parson

jilting his parish. What am I but this vibrating
branch? And who are you if not this lone

firefly quavering in a quiver of air? Quaver
on, Lord, quaver on. Nights like these,

of searching but not finding, I swear my body
is a garden where you play hide-n-seek,

now snuggling into my broken places, now
on the lam, coalescing into migrating clouds.

For weeks, I've been saying *Stay* (are you even
here?), weeks letting wind say my prayers.

After Reading Song of Songs, I Take Out the Garbage

My beloved is in a far country, which is to say
up thirteen carpeted stairs then hang
a quick left. I'm carrying into the cold
a bulging trash bag, big enough to hold
and hold and stretch and hold, like love itself,
and outfitted with handy draw strings.
The syllables of my beloved are sweeter
than the cherry yogurt that once brimmed
these cups, her clavicle sturdier than
corncobs, her skin fair as onion skins.
By now, she's stepping into the pools
of Solomon, or a mid-priced bath-shower
combo by Kohler, I know not which.
The moon is her luffa, with the Big Dipper
she spoons steaming water over her nakedness.
Or perhaps she is drying her hair with a spare
cat, seasoning her body with two hundred
shekels of saffron, one hundred each
of hyssop and camphor. Also a few shakes
of Johnson's baby powder. Perhaps the stars
are calling *Olly olly oxen free, join us in the sky.*
Please, My Beloved, flee not yet, stay a bit.
Are there children curled in your womb?
I toss away our collective trash and sniff . . .
Beyond the cul-de-sac a faint whiff of burning
forest. Two mountains away lies a lake,
trout jumping wave to wave. So too my zeal.
Half a dozen deer drift down from the foothills
to chew fallen pears. So too my hungry calm.
My kisses are like a breeze gentling sheets
on a clothesline, lazy and undulant.
I'll see your sycamores and firs, and raise
you rubies and a sea-green sapphire.

I've carried you. Will you carry me?
Lay me down upon your linens, lay us
both down. My ardor equals three ripe
pomegranates, yours a basket of tangerines.

Baedeker

Three blocks away from the Sistine Chapel, tucked
around a corner, sits a scruffy Roma girl selling

puppies. I've just come from Michelangelo's God,
rosy and scrubbed, splashed across a vaulted ceiling,

but his stretched hand still fails to calm Adam.
No chance back there to kneel on my prickly sins

or kiss a cherub's foot. Or sit. All I could do was
chastely stare. Here I can pick up and pet, cuddle

and kiss and snap grubby pictures with my phone.
The girl looks at me: *My papa he will drown them, yes.*

*In the big river. I must feed, yes. You take puppy, give
some little moneys?* Dirty sandals, unbrushed teeth.

She cradles a cup. Asks and asks, in two tongues
she asks, then pours a shiny whelp into my hands.

An Amateur's Guide to Holiness, Florence

Giotto's crucifix, *The Birth of Venus*, a Fra
Angelico in every lucky San Marco cell, *The David*,

not only the marble original but the copy
in the square when the sun hits it like doves,

the agony of Michelangelo's slaves trapped
in stone, a single muskrat paddling the Arno

like a prayerful pope, ten thousand lovers
padlocking erotic vows to the Ponte Vecchio,

the Duomo at dawn, twisting alleys before noon,
Dante at any hour, sparrows flitting in and out

of San Miniato al Monte while monks sing
a cappella to the dead, the drip drip of grotto

water in Boboli Gardens, the taste of blood
orange gelato at night on your wooing mouth.

Up to Their Dirty Wrists

They couldn't smuggle all of Saint Catherine's
body out of Rome, but part of her,
sure, that was worth a try. Didn't believers
throwing up prayers in Siena deserve
to place a piece of her in the basilica?
After breaching the grave, the robbers freed

her mummified head, without a blade,
without vertebrae snapping. Surely
that was a sign. And sneaking it past the sentry,
who looked straight into the heavy bag
but saw nothing but rose petals,
that was not only a sign but a miracle.

Rose petals in the dead of night, rose petals
the next morning, nine days of petals
during transport, Rome to Siena petals,
petals by horseback, petals over the shoulder,
stars resembling petals, petals when
the robbers gobbled stale bread, petals

when they peed, glory to God petals, lewd joke
petals, past cows and scrounging crows.
And still the thieves kept on: through silt
and salt, rain and ruin. What kind of petals?
Maybe dog rose or sweet briar or rosa mundi.
Wearily they trudged, no sleep to speak of,

their cargo forbidden but odiferous,
like scraps of paper. And when they plunged
their hands into that bag to bolster their faith,
petals up to their fingers, up to their dirty
wrists. No Thanatos here, only Eros.
Or so it felt crossing fields at midnight

under a beckoning moon. One day soon
they'd find a decaying head inside the bag,
one day Saint Catherine would haunt them,
but not tonight. They carried petals, petals
carried them, God's beasts of burden,
onward in the swoon of numinous perfume.

Happiness Memo

Meanwhile jumpy neighbor one has a gun range
bang bang in his basement and jumpy neighbor two

is chopping down pines to make room for pickle ball
meanwhile it's early October late afternoon

nothing I can do about it so I lie down on my lawn
and move my legs and arms as if it were Christmas

and I was inflicting a brave snow angel on my grass
meanwhile scads of geese angle south in little triangles

of travel meanwhile sky meanwhile I'm tired
when does Daylight Savings end I need that lost hour

meanwhile my daughter chalks a box on the drive
and her cat climbs in trapped in a spell of her own

broken purrs meanwhile leaves like letters fall
from on high each an invitation to an invisible prom

meanwhile a snake parting grass like the Red Sea
thinks croquet hoops are part of its pilgrimage

meanwhile my friend texts to say her liver cancer
is the good kind of terminal Selah and invites us

to dinner Selah and now the sun relaxes all over me
legs belly chest and creeps across my neck to lick

my face meanwhile a tow-headed kid rides by on a trike
his second lap pumpkin painted under one eye

skull under the other and shoots me with his finger
thus saving me the trouble Selah of getting back up

Waiting for a Visitation

Nothing to do but warm my hands over
the toaster and call it communion.
My superpower is laziness, so I laze.
My golden calf is a hammock swaying
beside a kettle lake, geese supplicating
water deities with each honk. I compose
lists. Favorite imported color: Loch Ness.
Favorite amusement park ride: melting
iceberg. If I ever write a post-apocalyptic
play, expect dripping water and kids
riding bikes around a smoldering fire.
Or maybe dripping fire and water riding
children around a bike. More chant
than talk, more hum than chant.
On buses, I toss my fingernails out
the window, hoping to offend local
gods. In lobbies, I pinch plastic flowers
just to be sure. At the end of each stanza,
I dangle my feet into white space
like a drunk hiker at Angels Landing.
Some call this cloud work, sudden
strokes of mojo, crows riding updrafts.
When I'm afraid, I close my eyes
and try to sing. When packages arrive,
I rip them open like a kid the day
before Christmas—no coded messages
from on high, no dark miracles
worth taking a bite of. I wait some more.

Book of Salt

For Dean Young (1955-2022)

I wanted to walk all over art, so I drove
    to *Spiral Jetty*. I wanted company,
        so I took a book of poems, *First Course
in Turbulence*, which promptly slipped

from my hand into the Great Salt Lake.
    I grabbed it before it sank, but it wrinkled
        badly, like a botched self-help book.
Seven times saltier than the sea—

a fascicle of tears. A few weeks later,
    at a signing, I passed that book
        to its author, who looked me over,
as if I'd tortured his first-born daughter

and wanted absolution. "I have felt,"
    he wrote, "like this book looks."
        His inscription was now the newest poem
in the collection. A backdoor jumping-off

point on how books are like people:
    moody, quick, perishable, frazzled
        at the edges! Not to mention salty.
So salty in fact, that I now keep

these poems in my spice rack.
    If a recipe calls for sea salt, I just rub
        the pages briskly, and—voila!—
Nature weeps into my chowder.

Lake Bonneville served up in a tureen.
    Which makes me an organic cook,
        a prophet of the sea. Also a docent
of love. Why? I took more than a book

of poems to *Spiral Jetty* that morning.
    I took my beloved. Or she took me.
        We kissed where the jetty ends, my
right hand holding wet poems,

my left stroking the small of her back.
    Vectors, vertigo, vortex. We settled into
        holding hands and greeted other pilgrims
drawing near. In the end, aren't we all odes

in search of other odes? Devotees drawn
    to mysteries that turn in on themselves,
        like a good treble clef, leaving us
stranded but praiseful, wet to our ankles,

in the middle of where we began.

Quail Egg

While watering, I found it under the Ponderosa pine,
a stray egg, already cold, dropped by a stray

hen in a hurry for better cover. A thing like that
you have to save, but my PJs had no pockets,

so I polished it on my sleeve and popped it
into the wet pouch of my mouth for safe keeping.

Its shell tasted like calcium, like sun, which is to say
like nothing at all. I moved that oval prayer

cheek to cheek, and even the names of my hostas—
Stained Glass, Blue Angel, Fire and Ice—

seemed to bear witness to a new magnetic north.
Was the egg fertilized? Should I call it a compass,

cook it in bacon fat? I felt old as an alderman, young
as rain. And for a moment, oppositions held:

tame/feral, spirit/flesh, me/not me, snail/sky.
Then Jacqui called from the kitchen for me

to grab a ripe peach or two, and the world wrinkled.
I answered in a nothing voice, like the groggy man

she'd kissed awake at dawn, but already I could taste
funerals on my tongue, wings unfolding at my back.

Acknowledgments

Thanks to the poetry editors of the following journals and magazines in which many of these poems first appeared:

32 Poems
Alpine Fellowship.com
Asheville Poetry Review
Beloit Poetry Journal
Bridport Prize Anthology 2023
Copper Nickel
Dalhousie Review
Diode
Five Points
Gettysburg Review
Gulf Coast
Hampden-Sydney Review
Image
Iowa Review Online
Kenyon Review
Lake Effect
London Magazine
Missouri Review Online
Missouri Review
New Letters
New Ohio Review
North American Review
Poetry International
Poetry Magazine
Poetry Northwest
Rattle
Smartish Pace
Southern Review
Tampa Review
Terrain.com

Two poems in this collection, "Having My Back Erased" and "Whatever Scared Hand," are part of a selection that won the 2023 Jeffrey E. Smith Editors' Prize sponsored by *Missouri Review*.

"This is Not the Hour of Poetry" placed first in the 2022 Alpine International Poetry Contest (England).

"Why I Kissed the Dead Man" placed third in the 2023 Bridport Competition (England).

"And Also I Ran" was a finalist in the 2020 *Rattle* Competition (USA), "Widow Water" a semi-finalist in 2021.

"Crickets Chirring" was a finalist in the 2023 Poetry International Competition (USA).

"Quail Egg" was reprinted in *Braving the Body* (2024).

Gracias to my better angels with whom I regularly break bread: Susan Howe, Michael Lavers, Scott Hatch, Steve Tuttle, and Spencer Hyde. Your candor and patience and snorts of laughter and irony and Netflix recommendations made it all possible.

Deep thanks to everyone at University of Tampa Press, especially Julie Nelson and Wesley Kapp, for their excellent work in midwifery, deep sea salvage, interior design, and jigsaw puzzles. And thanks to my editor and friend, Richard Mathews (1944-2024), for inviting me to the Tampa sock hop way back when.

Thanks to the College of Humanities and the English Department at Brigham Young University for providing me time to write, and to colleagues and students for keeping me honest.

Thanks as well to the following for their encouragement and incisive recommendations along the way: Jeff Levine, Kristina Marie Darling, Timothy Green, and Kylan Rice. And to my parents, who haunt these pages in a good way.

Special thanks to insomnia, which kept me grounded and writing in the wee hours, and to various contest judges for allowing me to briefly float.

All love poems—real, imagined or accidental—are dedicated to Jacqui Larsen.

About the Author

Former poet laureate of Utah, Lance Larsen grew up in the West mowing lawns, delivering newspapers, and dreaming of catching Bigfoot on film. He is the author of five previous poetry collections, all but one from University of Tampa. His work appears widely, in *New York Review of Books*, *The Times Literary Supplement*, *The Sun*, *London Magazine*, *APR*, *Best American Poetry*, and elsewhere. His awards include a Pushcart Prize, The *Tampa Review* Prize, The Jeffrey Smith Prize from *Missouri Review*, the *Sewanee Review* Prize, the *Swamp Pink* Prize, The Alpine Fellowship (England), and *The Moth* Poetry Prize (Ireland), as well as fellowships from Ragdale, The Anderson Center, and the National Endowment for the Arts. He teaches at Brigham Young University and likes to fool around with aphorisms: "When climbing a new mountain, wear old shoes." He is married to the painter and collage artist Jacqui Larsen. Sometimes he juggles.

About the Book

Making a Kingdom of It is set in Garamond Premier Pro digital fonts, based on original metal types by Claude Garamond and Robert Granjon that were designed and cast in Paris, France, in the sixteenth century. The book was designed and typeset by Wesley Kapp and Anika Schmid at the University of Tampa Press. The cover features artwork by Jacqui Larsen and was designed by Ana C. Alvarado Diaz.

www.ingramcontent.com/pod-product-compliance
Lightning Source LLC
Chambersburg PA
CBHW060538080526

44586CB00012B/794